Global Cities
BEIJING

Nancy Pellegrini
photographs by Adrian Cooper

Evans

Published by
Evans Brothers Limited,
Part of the Evans Publishing Group,
2A Portman Mansions
Chiltern Street
London WIU 6NR

First published 2007
© copyright Evans Brothers Limited

British Library Cataloguing in Publication Data

Pellegrini, Nancy
British Library Cataloguing in Publication Data

Pellegrini, Nancy
  Beijing. - (Global cities)
  1. Beijing (China) - Juvenile literature
  I. Title
  951.1'5606

ISBN-10: 0237531275
13-digit ISBN (from 1 January 2007) 978 0237 53127 0

Designer: Robert Walster, Big Blu Design
Maps and graphics by Martin Darlinson
All photographs are by Adrian Cooper/EASI-Images

Series concept and project management EASI –
Educational Resourcing
(info@easi-er.co.uk)

Contents

Living in an urban world

Some time in 2007, history is made. For the first time ever, the world's population becomes more urban than rural. An estimated 3.3 billion people are now living in towns and cities: for many, it's a fairly new experience. In China, for example, the number of people living in urban areas had increased from 196 million in 1980 to over 536 million by 2005.

The urban challenge...

The shift to a mainly urban population is being repeated across the world and provides a complex set of challenges for the twenty-first century. Many challenges are local: providing clean water for the people of expanding cities, for example. Other challenges are global. The spread of diseases in tightly packed cities is a problem, as it is between cities linked by air routes, high-speed trains and roads. Pollution from urban areas is another concern, as urban residents tend to generate more pollution than their rural counterparts.

▼ The position of Beijing in relation to China and, inset, other countries.

... and opportunity!

Urban centres, particularly major cities, also provide great opportunities for improving life. Cities can provide efficient forms of mass transport, such as subway or light rail networks. Services such as waste collection, recycling, education and healthcare can all work more efficiently in a city. Cities are centres of learning, and often the birthplace of new ideas. They provide a platform for arts and culture and, as their populations become more multicultural, these become increasingly global in their nature.

▼ The new Beijing of high-rise tower blocks and increasingly global influences looms large over one of the rapidly disappearing traditional networks of old lanes or *hutongs.*

A global city

Although all urban centres will share certain things in common, in some cities, the challenges and opportunities facing an urban world are particularly condensed. These are the world's global cities: they reflect the challenges of urbanisation, of globalisation, of citizenship and of sustainable development that face us all. Beijing is one of these cities, balancing being ruled by a secretive and powerful communist government whilst growing its economy and opening its markets to the world. Beijing is the cultural and political heart of the most populous nation on earth – its influence is hugely important. This book introduces you to the city and its people, and explores what makes Beijing a truly global city.

Beijing in China

Beijing, located in the centre of flat, dusty north China, was historically a centre of power, rather than a commercial city. For centuries, it was closed to foreigners (except invaders), and as a result, developed more slowly than the international trading cities of Shanghai and Guangzhou (Canton), with their links to Western countries. To China, holding power was always more important than making money. Now, while power is still important, Beijing wants to be rich too.

▶ Wealth and modernity are the important symbols of Beijing today as seen in the densely packed city centre viewed from the CCTV tower.

0   4 km

0   2 miles

5TH RING ROAD

Olympic Park

Summer Palace

Peking University

Kunming Lake

Zhongguancun

4TH RING ROAD

Dashanzi

3RD RING ROAD

Beijing North Station

Beijing Zoo

Confucian Temple

Dongzhimen

Wulu Station

WANGFUJING STREET

Jingshan Park

Dongcheng

Shijingshan

Yuyuan Lake

Zhongnanhai

Forbidden City

Temple Of The Sun

JINGTONG EXPRESSWAY

Gate of Heavenly Peace

Tiananmen Square

Beijing Station

Great Hall of The People

Chairman Mao Memorial

Beijing West Station

Fuxingmen

Beijing East Station

Peking Opera

Tiantan Park

Panjiayuan Market

Longtanhu Park

Tonghui River

Beijing South Station

3RD RING ROAD

4TH RING ROAD

Liangshui River

Legend

──── Main road

──── Major rail

� Park

▲ The centre of the city of Beijing.

10

Local challenge

Beijing's struggle to catch up economically, not only with the Western world, but also with other cities in China, has led to changes at breakneck speed. Like many cities in developing countries, Beijing has grown quickly, creating problems such as pollution, serious water shortages, and traffic. The city has many old buildings, but is tearing down its traditional architecture for the sake of modernity. Property developers and business people are getting rich, buying luxury cars and expensive houses, but many homes still lack adequate heating or plumbing. There is a significant, visible underclass, riding through the city in mule carts, or piled together in the back of pickup trucks. A shortage of essential resources, an economically divided population, and increasing conflict between traditional values and modern life are all issues facing Beijing in the twenty-first century.

▲ Beijing sits in the middle of an agricultural area that is rapidly disappearing as the city develops and expands at an incredible rate.

Beijing Facts

Name: Beijing Municipality, one of four municipalities in China (not attached to any province)

Location: North China, surrounded by Hebei Province

Area: 16,808 sq km

Population: (2005) 11-15 million, including 3.7 million registered migrants

County-level divisions: 16 districts, 2 counties

Language: Beijing dialect, basis of standard Mandarin Chinese

The history of the city

Beijing has existed as far back as the Zhou Dynasty (1122-221 BC), when it was a trade outpost for Koreans, Mongols and tribes from Central China. Since then, Beijing has been invaded, flattened, rebuilt, invaded again, and served as capital of five different dynasties, as well as of modern day China. The city's history has been a constant struggle between Chinese and foreign elements, or the Chinese against each other.

▶ The Great Wall of China was begun in around 221 BC to deter invaders from Central Asia from reaching Chinese strongholds, including Beijing, to the south.

Before Beijing

Beijing (then called Ji) was the capital of the Liao (916-1125 AD) and Jin Dynasties (1115-1234) of northern China, before Mongol invaders from the north burned it to the ground after a seven-year siege. Ji then became Dadu, the capital of the Mongol Yuan Dynasty (1279-1368), the builders of the famous *hutongs*, or the narrow winding lanes that make up modern Beijing's poorer neighbourhoods and also its most popular tourist attractions.

The Yuan Dynasty united China, but financial problems and natural disasters led to its collapse, allowing the Ming Dynasty to return China to Chinese control. Emperor Yong Le designed the modern layout of the city, now renamed Beijing. At the centre of Beijing was built the Imperial Palace, or Forbidden City, that was off-limits to the masses. A north-south axis

◀ An elaborately carved walkway in Beijing's Forbidden City. Once strictly off-limits, the Forbidden City is today one off the major tourist attractions in Beijing.

bisects the central area, while the rest of the city is in a grid format, with *hutongs* connecting the main roads.

Beijing (and China) was not in Chinese hands for long. New northern invaders (the Manchus) stormed the capital. The new Manchu Qing Dynasty (1644-1912) expanded Beijing, restored old buildings and constructed new ones – most notably the Summer Palace in the north west of the city.

The twentieth century

By the late nineteenth century, wars and lavish spending by its rulers had weakened the country, allowing foreign powers to establish a military and commercial presence. The Chinese reacted to the unpopular foreign presence with the 'Boxer Rebellion' of 1900. The Boxers were a martial arts group who initially opposed the Qing Dynasty, until they decided foreigners were the greater evil. The Boxers occupied Beijing with over 140,000 soldiers, holding the foreign community hostage for over two months. An alliance of eight foreign powers, known as the Eight Power Alliance, crushed the rebellion, rescued the hostages, and forced the ruling Dowager Empress Cixi to sign the humiliating Boxer Protocol treaty, forcing the Chinese to pay huge sums in reparations. This treaty is still a source of shame to the Chinese, and is one root of widespread distrust of foreigners today.

▲ Visitors roam amongst the remains of the first Summer Palace, which was destroyed by French and British troops in the 1860s.

Civil unrest

After the overthrow of the Qing in 1912, warlords overran the capital, and Japanese forces invaded China from the east. In 1918 the government secretly ceded nearby Shandong Province to Japan, and when the treaty became known there were massive student protests. These protests were called the 4 May Movement (1919), and its leaders established principles of socialism the Chinese Communist Party would later adopt as their own. Without a strong central government, China became prey to competing and violent political groups. The Chinese Communist Party (CCP), led by Mao Zedong (1893-1976) spent the 1920s and 1930s fighting the right-wing Kuomintang Party (KMT) led by Chiang Kai-shek (1887-1975). When these two groups weren't fighting each other, they fought independent warlords, and the Japanese, who, after colonising northeast China, occupied Beijing in 1937. After the surrender of the Japanese at the end of the Second World War in 1945, the CCP and KMT conflict became known as the Chinese Civil War.

◀ A giant portrait of Mao Zedong, China's most influential communist leader, hangs above Wumen Gate of the Forbidden City.

Mao Zedong

When Mao Zedong's Communist army marched through the countryside, he ordered his soldiers not to loot any homes, which helped to recruit a wave of grateful farmers. Mao defeated the KMT with his 'peasant revolution' in 1949, and established his capital in Beijing. Over two million defeated KMT fled to the island of Taiwan, taking money and cultural treasures with them – which mainlanders still want back. Overseas Chinese returned to the 'New China', which promised to become a united, prosperous, and peaceful nation. Unfortunately, the next fifty years saw tremendous poverty, and little peace.

In the 1950s the government launched an 'anti-rightist campaign' to rid the country of non-Communist influences, targeting artists, writers, intellectuals and wealthy landowners. Following the anti-rightist campaign was the

'Great Leap Forward' (1958-60) – a programme designed to rapidly develop industry and agriculture simultaneously, which instead created a nationwide famine between 1960 and 1962 and the death of up to 30 million peasants.

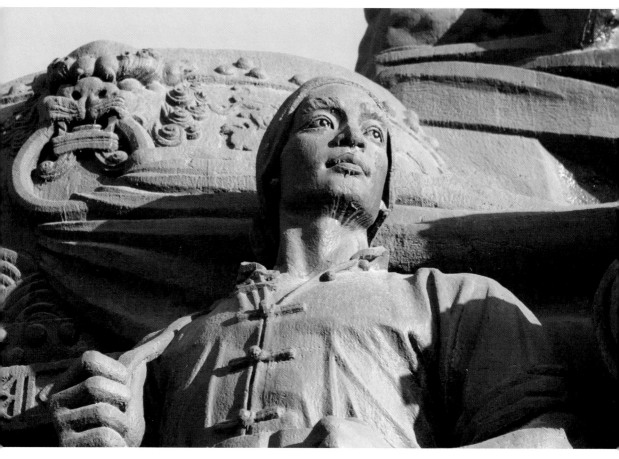

▲ A sculpture at Beijing's National Agricultural Exhibition Centre depicts rural workers during the Cultural Revolution era, when farming was an honoured profession.

More civil unrest

The next large programme introduced by the Communist leadership was called the Cultural Revolution (1966-76), which once again attempted to eradicate China of non-Communist thinking. Soldiers, factory workers and farmers were the honoured professions, while professors, engineers and scientists were sacked, sent to labour camps, imprisoned or even killed. Beijing's schools, libraries and universities were closed, and urban teenagers were sent to work on farms, far from the city – sometimes for as long as ten years.

Other students formed militia groups called 'Red Guards', each claiming undying loyalty to Mao Zedong. The Red Guards swept through the city, destroying temples and monuments, arresting citizens, confiscating property, and fighting, and even killing each other. Neighbours informed on neighbours, students on teachers, and children on parents, and a generation of Chinese grew up without an education. This chaos, lawlessness and abandonment of traditional values did lasting damage to society.

After Mao

Mao Zedong died in 1976, and the next important leader to follow him was Deng Xiaoping, in 1978. Deng reopened the universities and reinstated the dismissed intellectuals and government officials. Most importantly, he gradually changed China to a market economy. The government no longer decided what people could eat, where they could live, or what career they chose. For the first time making money was allowed and became more important than politics.

▼ The gradual opening up of China following Mao's death in 1976 has led to the emergence of wealth as a status symbol.

Massacre

In May 1989, students and workers gathered in Tiananmen Square in central Beijing to protest against government corruption and growing social inequalities. On 4 June the protest was violently crushed by the Chinese military, which killed thousands of protesters – exact figures are not known as the Chinese government will not release them. Horrified foreign nations severed economic and diplomatic ties with China, resulting in a decrease in trade, investment, and education abroad.

Smaller political protests had occurred before but the Tiananmen unrest changed how people felt about their government –

Beijing residents today have less faith in the government and the Communist Party. The Tiananmen event also taught the Chinese that they were no longer an isolated nation – the world was watching. International opinion suddenly became extremely important to the Chinese, from the authorities down to ordinary citizens. When China joined the World Trade Organisation (WTO) in 2000 and Beijing won the right to host the 2008 Olympics many observers felt that China was being readmitted to international affairs. During the Tang Dynasty (618-907), China was the world leader; now many Chinese feel that China is becoming the leader again.

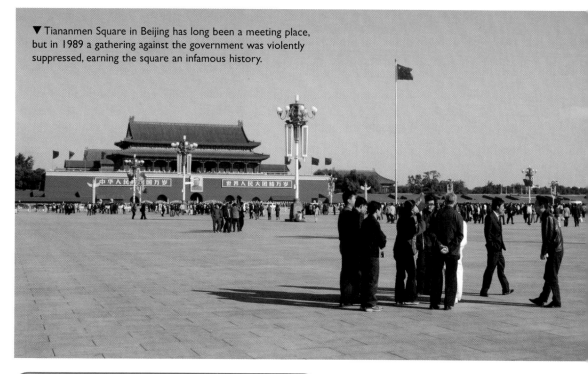

▼ Tiananmen Square in Beijing has long been a meeting place, but in 1989 a gathering against the government was violently suppressed, earning the square an infamous history.

CASE STUDY

Chen Mei remembers Mao's China

Corporate training consultant Chen Mei was still a child when Mao Zedong died in 1976, but she remembers a different Beijing: blue skies, empty, safe streets, and friendly people. "It has something to do with equality," she says. "Back then, you could be a street sweeper, or a university professor, your lives were the same. Today everyone wants more."

But in those days, people worked together. "My mum was a doctor," Chen says, herself a mother of two. "She used to steal bandages and alcohol, and then swap them with other mums who worked in grocery stores, to get meat or vegetables." In those days, Beijing operated on a rationing system – the government issued tickets for limited supplies of meat, oil, sugar, rice, and other necessities. This was confusing, however, for a child whose teachers kept talking about honesty. "I used

to blame my mum," Chen says, "But I didn't understand life. Foreigners wonder how people survived on seven dollars a year, but that's how we survived. It was a community."

The people of Beijing

As China's capital, and one of its most developed areas, Beijing is a magnet for the rural unemployed and 'out-of-province' people who live a semi-legal existence in the city. China has a gigantic population – the same as the US, Indonesia, Brazil, Pakistan, Bangladesh, Russia, Nigeria, Japan, the UK and France combined. A population this big puts massive pressure on resources, jobs, and university places. This causes resentment among Beijingers towards the rural disadvantaged, who are just looking for a better life.

▲ As Beijing continues to develop, overcrowding, traffic congestion and air pollution are among the challenges facing the city and its people.

Crowded Beijing

Beijing is China's largest city in area, its municipality measuring 16,808 sq km, just slightly smaller than the state of Kuwait. It has a population density across the entire metropolitan area of 888 people per sq km. However, the central area's seven million live on only 1,369 sq km, raising the density in the middle of the city to 7,570 people per sq km. Even as the city spreads outwards, the centre becomes more crowded.

People need places to live, to eat, to work, relax and to shop, and the booming construction industry brings money to the local economy. However many new apartments remain empty, because no one can afford them – yet. Road traffic is increasing, while clean air and water are rapidly diminishing, and the crowds and noise can be intolerable.

Moving people

Planners are preparing 'Beijing of 2020' – an 18-million resident megalopolis combining the urban centre, suburbs, and 11 satellite cities (see p 57). This will require people to leave their homes as sites are redeveloped. Developers evict some residents under protest or by force; others voluntarily move to find jobs in the hi-tech industries, factories, universities and schools being built in the new cities. Developers are also building luxury apartments in the northern Hui Long Guan and Tian Tong Yuan areas, to lure the wealthy to create affluent suburbs.

▲ Housing for government workers is demolished in the Sanlitun area to make way for a new development consisting of a shopping centre and restaurants.

One Child Policy

A controversial consequence of China's staggering population size is the One Child Policy, established in 1979, that limits couples to one child. Since the founding of 'New China' (the PRC) in 1949, the population has increased by around 700 million. The policy is an attempt to arrest this huge growth in population. It applies only to the majority urban Han Chinese, but not to rural Chinese, ethnic minorities (China has 56 ethnic groups), couples where both partners were only children, or those married to foreigners. The policy was

established as a temporary, emergency measure, and today even the tightly controlled official media is suggesting the benefits of a two-child policy instead.

▼ Beijing population growth 1950-2015

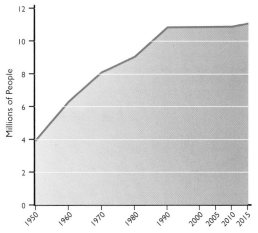

▼ A grandfather cares for his only grandchild on the southern outskirts of the city. The one-child policy dramatically reduced China's population growth, but may be phased out in the future.

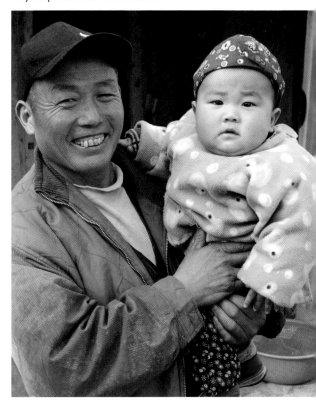

The 'out of Beijing' population

Beijing has a large migrant population, but rather than having migrants from abroad, as in many other global cities, migrants in Beijing come from within China. Some of these migrants are from ethnic minorities and some from the majority Han Chinese.

▲ Migrant workers carrying their possessions in tarpaulin bags arrive at the Dongzhimen bus station. Many rural migrants arrive in Beijing in this way, hoping to find work.

Hukous

Before potential migrants can move around China they need a *hukou*, or residency permit. Beijing is very attractive to migrants for its educational and job opportunities, even if taking up those opportunities means leaving families behind. For this reason the city government makes it hard for outer-province students to get *hukous* and attend universities in Beijing; the government feels that after they graduate, they'll add to the city's permanent population.

Getting a *hukou* is not a guarantee of finding work, and well-paid jobs may be hard to find. In order to prevent out-of-work migrants causing trouble, the Beijing authorities try to find the new migrants

▲ A resident shows his *hukou* or residency permit – the pass necessary to access almost anything in Beijing.

work of any kind, no matter how trivial – leading to many people getting jobs that seem pointless: bored subway attendants rip passenger tickets, and throw both halves away; office supply stores have different clerks for pens, paper, and notebooks (shoppers have to bring their receipts to the cash register and then go back to collect their purchase); and security guards are everywhere, guarding nothing.

Life of migrants

The China Daily newspaper puts Beijing's average salary at US$466 per month; Beijingers claim it's about US$248. Unskilled migrant workers, such as waiting staff and construction workers, can expect to earn as little as US$30-60 monthly – low by the standards of ordinary Beijingers, but higher than in the migrants' home provinces. Many low-salary workers live in military-style dormitories, or tarpaulin tents, and have little access to medical care or education. Construction workers are usually only paid once a year before the Chinese New Year, when they traditionally travel back to their homes. Sometimes crooked bosses run away with the money before pay day, leaving the workers penniless, but the government is cracking down on such practices.

Hundreds of thousands of Koreans, Europeans, and North Americans study or work in Beijing – Beijingers often resent the disproportionately high wages these people earn, but feel that English teachers and international business people will help China's development.

▶ Migrant construction workers from Henan Province in their sleeping and living quarters. These men have been hired to build the stadium that will hold the Olympics in Beijing in 2008.

While all of China's fifty-six ethnic groups are represented in Beijing, these groups have the largest membership.

Ethnic Group Breakdown in Beijing, according to 2000 Census

Group (nationality)	Number	Percentage
Han Chinese	12,983,696	95.69
Manchu	250,286	1.84
Hui	235,837	1.74
Mongol	37,464	0.28
Korean / Chinese	20,369	0.15
Tujia	8372	0.062
Zhuang	7322	0.054
Miao	5291	0.039
Uyghur	3129	0.023
Tibetan	2920	0.022

Living in Beijing

With its population of over 15 million people, Beijing is China's second largest city, after Shanghai. Most of the population is from the ethnic Han majority group, but small pockets of ethnic minorities exist. With its strong central government and position as China's most important cultural and political centre, Beijing has had investment in healthcare and education, but with its huge growth in population in the last 50 years the pressures on such services have become almost intolerable.

▶ The outpatient department of the Peking Union Hospital.

Healthcare

Hospitals in Beijing are better than almost anywhere else in China, and many Western-style facilities meet international standards, but healthcare is expensive. Doctors are underpaid and unsatisfied, and the hospitals are very crowded.

Government and multinational company employees get some reimbursement for medical bills, but actual health insurance is nonexistent. Patients must bring cash deposits of over US$1,000 in value to secure hospital treatment, even for emergency care. This is one reason why China has a personal savings rate of about 40 per cent of income, compared to one per cent in the USA.

Another problem is the lack of primary care – sometimes patients needing non-emergency care must have *guanxi* (connections) to see a doctor at all. By developing country standards, Beijing does have a high rate of doctors to patients – 1.6 per 1000 (India only has 0.4 per 1000), but China as a whole needs a half million new doctors to bring services up to a Western standard. Doctors are well respected but they must work long, high-pressure hours for low pay. Surgeons are the best-paid doctors, but earn only about US$700 a month – including bribes from the patients' family. Foreign English language teachers working half the hours earn twice as much money. Many disgusted doctors are leaving the profession, preferring to work in medical supply sales, patent offices, or even the travel industry.

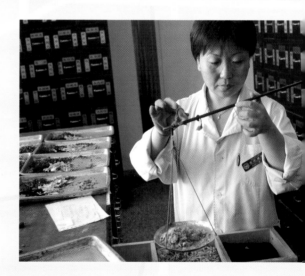

▲ Prescriptions for traditional Chinese medicines are carefully weighed out in a Beijing hospital. Herbal remedies continue to play a major role in Chinese healthcare.

▲ Medical staff discuss patient care at the Bayley and Jackson Medical Centre, a private healthcare clinic that mainly caters to the expatriate community.

SARS

The Severe Acute Respiratory Syndrome (SARS) outbreak of 2003 originated in southern China. Quickly carried around the world by air transport, it caused deaths in Singapore, Hong Kong, Vietnam, Canada, and hit Beijing especially hard. As the transport hub of China, SARS was carried in by migrant workers and spread through the city. Residents resorted to wearing facemasks and boiling vinegar to purify the air; schools closed, restaurants were deserted, and checkpoints to check people's body temperature were set up outside buildings and on highways. Accurate statistics are unavailable, but hundreds of Chinese died, and thousands were infected.

The city authorities were accused of covering up the extent of the problem, but since then important lessons have been learnt: that disease spreads rapidly through a country of 1.3 billion people, that secrecy damages credibility, and that epidemics harm the national economy – the tourism industry lost US$2.4 billion in two months. Learning from SARS, China has adopted aggressive policies for dealing with HIV/AIDS, involving education programs, free testing and even needle exchange.

▶ A pedestrian considers an HIV/AIDS awareness poster in a subway passage.

Education

Beijing schools use a system of learning based on rote memorisation where authority is unquestioned. This results in millions of students who struggle to express their opinions. This hurts Chinese working in international companies, and even in China, as students do not develop creativity and problem-solving skills.

School classes can have between 40 and 60 students, which makes it hard for teachers to give individual attention where it is needed. Teachers are often blamed for poor student performance, so will often try and raise standards by shaming under-performing children. Primary school goes from age six to 12, middle school from 13 to 15, and high school for 16 to 18, with entrance exams at every level. Students can win academic or athletic scholarships to the better out-of-district schools. In addition to the 251-day school year (the world's longest), most take *ke wai* – extra weekend or holiday classes. These and school fees make the 'free' education very expensive – many parents say they couldn't afford more than one child, even if there wasn't a One Child Policy.

Beijing students tend to stay in the same group for years, and they often form close relationships that continue long after graduation, and may even help future job opportunities. Students also develop emotional security – there are few problems with bullying in Beijing schools.

◀ Students enjoy an art class at a middle school in Dongzhimen.

The *Gao Kao*

Students at the top schools can better prepare for the *gao kao*, or university entrance exam, the result of which determines their university, course of study and their future job success. A child in a good university can mean financial security for the family, so studying is a group effort. Parents sometimes give up their jobs to monitor their children's progress; grandparents may attend lectures, sneaking in tape recorders or taking notes. Some children breathe in pure oxygen (from special bars) for energy, the parents of others rent homes closer to school. The Beijing government stops construction near testing centres months before the exam, and parents lobby their apartment complexes to stop excess noise.

The *gao kao*, besides adding pressure to the lives of students, also prevents education reform. The government does try to free teachers from the rigid curriculum and encourage more classroom 'democracy', but as parents worry so much about *gao kao* results the system is hard to change. One advantage of the system is its legitimacy – in a city where street vendors sell university diplomas outside railway stations, the *gao kao* is a more valid sign of academic achievement.

▲ A student checks notice-boards at the Peking University campus. Peking University is Beijing's premier university and places are highly prized.

Preserving old Beijing

In the past Beijing was a flat city with one-storey courtyard housing called *siheyuans*, along winding *hutongs* (lanes). Some *siheyuans* are over 800 years old, most lack kitchens, bathrooms and central heating, and their coal stoves make Beijing's pollution even worse. Despite their often primitive living conditions, however, many people consider them the heart of the city. Unfortunately their central location is ideal

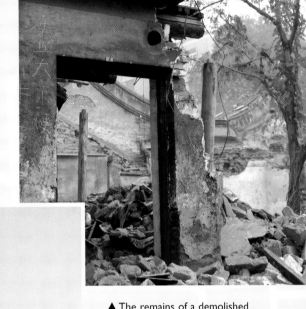

▲ The remains of a demolished *hutong* with a tree standing in what would have been the courtyard. Many of the *hutongs* in Beijing have met a similar fate in the name of modernisation and development.

for the building of high-priced apartments and tearing them down is easier than preserving them for the future.

Some feel that the houses are no longer fit for habitation, but residents claim they can be renovated for as little as US$3,000. Unfortunately, Mao's land redistribution programmes destroyed all records of their ownership, leaving hutong dwellers locked in uncertain legal battles with aggressive and well-funded developers.

◀ Tourism could be the saviour of the hutong in Beijing. This *hutong* residency has been converted into a restaurant. Others have become trendy bars.

Hutong life

Hutongs foster good citizenship in a way impersonal high-rise buildings cannot, as residents meet each other in the course of their day. Residents run dry cleaners, tailors or even small restaurants out of their homes – relocating means a loss of livelihood as well as community. Children play in the quiet streets away from traffic, and the elderly get the social contact they need. Even young professionals feel insulated from Beijing's chaos. The Beijing authorities are experimenting with solutions, such as encouraging local government and residents to work together in creating an economically sustainable neighbourhood.

▲ Beijing's *hutongs* are a stark contrast to the congestion, noise and pollution of the modern city and provide for a better quality of community life.

CASE STUDY

Ding Ai, *hutong* preservation activist

"How will we know where we came from?" asks Ding Ai, *hutong* preservation activist. "You know you came from your mother, and she came from her mother. If we destroy the city's history, how will we know where we came from?" When Ding found her house branded with the character *chai* (destroy), she sprang into action. Knowing she had only thirty days to vacate her family home, she hired architects and engineers who submitted affidavits, swearing to its structural integrity, then she promised to renovate. She succeeded in saving her home.

Now Ding wants to save the city. "Everything in the old city is gold," she says. "And the area is so small already, why do they have to make it smaller?" She campaigns for clearer property laws, lobbies to protect historical areas, and writes articles for newspapers and journals. "Foreigners don't want to fly on a plane for

fifteen hours to see tall buildings, they can see them at home," she scoffs. "Without the *hutongs*, it's not Beijing." She acknowledges that government is working on solutions, but also that people move faster than laws. "*Hutongs* get torn down every day," she says sadly, "there's no time."

The survival of tradition

China's long history has created a tradition of spectacular and unusual crafts, and craftspeople continue work their families have done for generations. But China's fascination with rapid development and conspicuous consumption has would-be artisans choosing careers in engineering or information technology, and traditional crafts are struggling to survive.

▼ Hi-tech skills such as computer engineering are in much greater demand by today's youth than traditional skills.

Chinese claim to be very proud of their craft history, but chose to spend their money on computer games, i-pods, or new cars instead, leaving these multi-generational craftspeople struggling. Another problem is that during the Cultural Revolution, all traditional activities were prohibited, and a whole generation of parents never taught their children about their history. Some Beijingers are starting culture schools, hoping Chinese will learn their own cultural traditions, and teach foreigners in Beijing. Others hope that government will give tax breaks or subsidies to artists preserving China's culture, but this seems unlikely in the near future. Like *hutongs* and *siheyuans*, traditional crafts have to depend on the tourist trade and foreign interest.

▼ Modern global brands and growing consumerism threaten the survival of many traditional crafts and industries in Beijing.

Crafts

Skilled craftspeople carve elaborate sculpture using ice (*bingdiao*), play dough (*miansu*) or even butter (*suyouhua*). Hair embroidery (*faxiu*) is especially difficult, since hair is more brittle than silk. Microscopic carving (*weidao*) is usually done on ivory or a single strand of human hair – artisans must feel with their fingers only. Shanghai's Zhang Yunhu reproduced the entire CPC Constitution (14,000 characters) on a chip of ivory only 2.8 square centimetres, about the size of a postage stamp – visible only under 100x magnification.

Tang Yujie, crafts maker

"Every country has its good points," says Tang Yujie, owner of Bannerman Tang's Toys and Handicrafts. "Western countries have developed technology, China has a traditional culture. I want the world to know the real China." The Tang family is descended from high-level Qing Dynasty officials, and has been

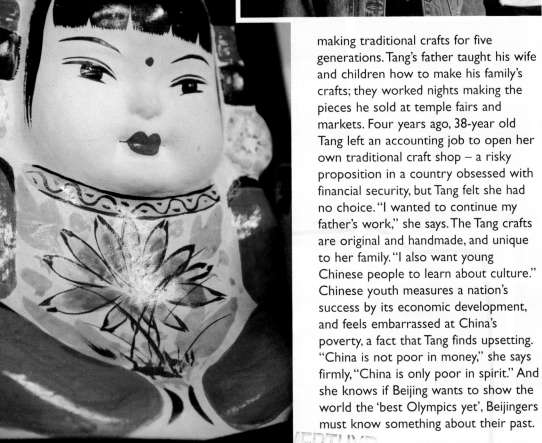

making traditional crafts for five generations. Tang's father taught his wife and children how to make his family's crafts; they worked nights making the pieces he sold at temple fairs and markets. Four years ago, 38-year old Tang left an accounting job to open her own traditional craft shop – a risky proposition in a country obsessed with financial security, but Tang felt she had no choice. "I wanted to continue my father's work," she says. The Tang crafts are original and handmade, and unique to her family. "I also want young Chinese people to learn about culture." Chinese youth measures a nation's success by its economic development, and feels embarrassed at China's poverty, a fact that Tang finds upsetting. "China is not poor in money," she says firmly, "China is only poor in spirit." And she knows if Beijing wants to show the world the 'best Olympics yet', Beijingers must know something about their past.

The city economy

Overseas investment in China's economy has driven it from global insignificance to the world's fourth largest in just 25 years, with an annual growth rate of 9.9 per cent in 2005 (the UK's measured at 1.7 per cent). Beijing accounts for 3.1 per cent (US$51.4 billion) of this growth; this investment in the capital means more manufacturing, and a growth in investment in the city infrastructure, hi-tech industries, and large scale environmental projects.

▶ The China World Trade Centre building is symbolic of the expansion in international trade for both Beijing and China.

China's trade

China's 1.3 billion people create both the world's largest single market and the planet's cheapest labour force. Foreign companies relocate their factories, pay less for workers and materials, and sell their goods for a higher profit back home. The Chinese want to be more than the world's factory – by insisting that foreign and Chinese companies work in joint-ventures, they ensure China develops to fully compete in a globalised world.

◀ China's is the world's largest consumer market but wages are so low that few can afford to shop in luxury malls such as this.

▼ Contribution to Beijing's economy by sector.

Manufacturing
26%

Services
62.4%

Financial
11.6%

Beijing's industries

Foreign investors appreciate Beijing's reputation for safety and stability, as well as the rapid development and the international credibility the 2008 Olympics has created. Today, multinationals establish both regional headquarters and research and development (R & D) centres in special economic zones, such as Central Business District (CBD) and Finance Street. Zhongguancun, Beijing's Silicon Valley and its brightest economic star, is home to 8000 hi-tech industries and Microsoft and Motorola are among the 20-plus multinationals to establish R & D centres there.

Manufacturing is still Beijing's largest single industry, providing 88.6 per cent of its total industrial output value. Beijing is also expanding its auto industry, which is located in outlying suburban districts such as Tongzhou, Miyun and Huairou.

▲ The foreign director of an animal feed factory meets Chinese businessmen at a sales conference on the outskirts of Huairou district in Beijing. International partnerships are an important aspect of Beijing's economic growth.

CASE STUDY

Shaan Price, party organiser

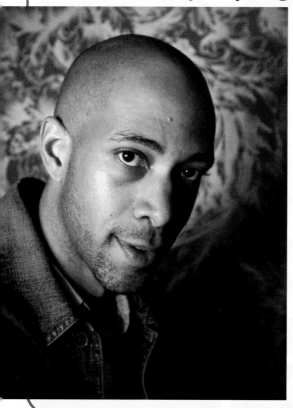

Since coming to Beijing from the USA, Shaan Price has modelled, taught English, worked for both UNESCO and an import-export company, and has a large role in the film *Muo Gong*, or *Battle of Wits*. But parties are what come naturally. "It started as just a way to get all my Chinese and foreign friends together," he says, of his first nightclub-sized birthday event, "and I wanted to raise money for a local orphanage." His guests never knew that their drinks paid for an orphan's cleft-palate surgery.

The owners of a local nightclub were impressed by Price's social contacts, and offered him a partnership, in exchange for his design and business ideas. But business relationships with Chinese can be challenging. "There is little trust of foreigners, or even other Chinese," he explains. "And the drive for money is so strong, you can feel it." As for success in Beijing, he says "You need a creative eye, and the drive to try something new."

Government work

In 1978, Deng Xiaoping said "To get rich is glorious." His words turned an enormous socialist economy upside down. During Mao's time, private enterprise had been illegal, and everyone worked for the State. *Danweis*, or work units, provided workers with their food, clothing, housing, work and pensions, as well as controlling their personal lives – marriage, divorce, even childbirth. *Danweis* still nominally exist, but gone are the guaranteed jobs and benefits of the State Owned Enterprise (SOE) system. Today's Chinese must learn to provide for themselves.

Unemployment

Drastically slashing the SOE workforce helped Beijing's sluggish economy, but it left many middle-aged workers without work. Having grown up during the Cultural Revolution, they lacked the skills and education to be competitive. Beijing's official unemployment level hovers at 2.5 per cent but the real number is probably higher. Educated Beijingers feel government jobs are boring and poorly paid, with advancement impossible without proper *guanxi* (connections). Most want to work abroad, or for multinational joint-ventures, where connections aren't important and the pay is better.

▼ Government employees collect tickets on the Beijing subway. Where once everyone worked for the government, private employment is becoming the norm today.

Bilingual Beijing

This globalisation of Beijing has created another sector of the economy – Teaching of English as a Foreign Language, or TEFL. Having an English-speaking Beijing work force means the high-priced foreigners would no longer be needed, and would leave more international companies in local hands. A bilingual Beijing is also a viable alternative to Indian cities for Western outsourcing of industries like call centres. Beijingers can learn Western medical, technological, research and management techniques abroad; the ones who stay away send back money, others, called *hai gui* (sea turtles), return home to make the most of their new skills in the growing economy.

The upcoming 2008 Beijing Olympics is an important catalyst for English education. The Beijing Organising Committee of the Olympic Games (BOCOG) has plans for the 'Best Olympics in World History', that go beyond traffic management or stadium construction to bilingual volunteers. "To foreigners, you represent China," says the directive, "to Chinese you represent Beijing." Even taxi drivers are supposed to be studying from their 'taxi English' book, though drivers rarely have the courage to practise with foreigners.

▲ Students practise their English conversation at one of the many language schools in Beijing. The ability to speak English is considered essential to career success, particularly amongst younger people.

Informal economy

Of course, not every worker needs English. Beijing also has an extensive informal economy, made up of 'out of Beijing' people. Every neighbourhood has bicycle repairmen, tailors, cobblers, and key makers who work on the sidewalks, and fruit vendors who sell out of mule carts. Recyclers sift through rubbish bins for cardboard or bottles, or steal metal manhole covers from the street. Vendors squat on pedestrian bridges selling jewellery, hair clips, stolen books, and fake telephone cards. And pirate DVDs are everywhere – on sidewalks, in black canvas bags, and in small, clearly labelled shops with blaring music – US$1 for a movie, US$8 for a whole television series.

▼ A man waits for passing trade at his mobile key cutting and bicycle repair store. Such enterprises are a familiar part of Beijing's informal economy.

▲ The main Olympic stadium for the 2008 games under construction in 2006. The Olympics have led to a massive construction boom in the city.

Urban renewal

The 2008 Olympics' massive construction boom is giving rise to stadiums, apartment complexes, and even a National Theatre. Beijing's urban renewal is visible everywhere. Places like Sanlitun and Houhai were low-income residential areas that changed into fashionable nightspots. Even south Beijing, usually dismissed as 'poor', is attracting a class of young, upwardly mobile Chinese. But the most dramatic shift in land use has seen abandoned military factories turned into centres for the creation and selling of contemporary art by local Chinese artists.

▲ 'Photo 798' is one of the art galleries that has contributed to the regeneration of Dashanzi, a former industrial area of Beijing.

Factory galleries

After the military abandoned the buildings, the high-ceilinged ex-factories of places like Dashanzi, with their large windows and natural light were perfect for Beijing's fledgling art community. Foreign collectors have paid as much as US$412,775 for contemporary Chinese works. With the art gallery boom came coffee shops restaurants, and offices for designers and publishers.

Poor artists have a way of creating trendy neighbourhoods. Dashanzi is no exception, except with one Chinese twist – this area has become so valuable, it's now threatened with demolition. Dashanzi straddles the corridor between the city and the airport, making it an ideal place for luxury high-rises or an expansion of Zhongguancun. Artists have successfully petitioned to preserve the area until after the Olympics, but once the games are over no-one knows what will happen.

Many feel that creative zones like Dashanzi are important to a city that wants to evolve beyond being a global manufacturing centre. Another important issue is intellectual property; China is notorious for copying, pirating, or counterfeiting design ideas and products from other countries, and may only stop when its own inventions and products are threatened.

CASE STUDY

Song Zhuang – an artist community

In 1995, a group of ten artists clustered in hovels around Yuanmingyuan, the ruins of the first Summer Palace, before they were driven out. Today, those ten artists have evolved into Song Zhuang, the world's largest art community, with 500 artists living in villages just outside Dashanzi. "Back then, the government control over art was very tight," says Sally Liu, owner of the Artist Village Gallery. "You couldn't have an exhibition, the police would come and shut it down. But today, the government gets financial benefit from this community," she continues. When Liu took a neighbourhood landfill and turned it into a successful gallery, she tripled the property values of the neighbouring homes.

"It's the most active group for experimental art," says Liu, "and the only one with such a long history." Artists come from all over China, attracted by the fame of former Song Zhuang members that have become art celebrities. But Sally Liu doesn't think about fame. "I try to help those who are not famous, but who are very talented," says Liu. "Emerging artists."

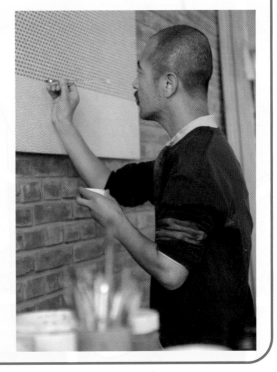

▶ An artist at work in the Song Zhuang community.

Managing Beijing

China's 9.6 million square kilometres is divided into various zones of government – there are 22 provinces, five Autonomous Regions, and two Special Autonomous Regions, with an average population of 45.3 million each. Beijing, however, is one of China's four municipalities – cities under central government control (the others are Shanghai, Chongqing and Tianjin). As China's seat of national government, Beijing has some special challenges.

The Beijing municipal government

The Beijing municipal government controls China's largest (in landmass) city. Beijing is comprised of two counties and sixteen districts – four urban, four suburban, and eight outlying suburban districts. The city government's six major departments oversee such functions as education, economics and development, science and technology, and ethnic and minority affairs, as well as security and general administration.

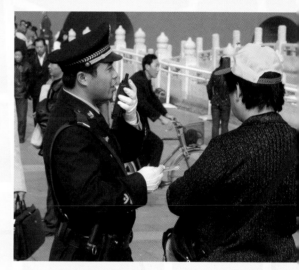

▲ A police officer checks the papers of a street trader in front of the Forbidden City.

Law enforcement

The most visible department is the Public Security Bureau (PSB), essentially Beijing's police force. However, besides dealing with criminals, riots, prisons and traffic safety, the PSB handles fire fighting, provides security to government agencies and visiting guests of the state, and overseas travel and residency affairs for citizens, migrants and foreigners. The PSB also must 'have full knowledge of the elements affecting policy stability, harming domestic security and disrupting public order'. Secret groups are automatically suspect in China – for example, although Beijing has plenty of churches, Christian groups meeting at private homes may have been visited by the PSB. Citizens have the right to belong to a religion, but it must be officially sanctioned.

▲ An officer in the Beijing Fire Department demonstrates equipment during an open day held at the Forbidden City to encourage public awareness in fire safety.

The Communist Party of China (CPC)

At one time, the Party controlled people's work, homes, marriage, children and success. Outstanding elementary school students became Young Pioneers; studious teenagers joined the Youth League, and eighteen year-olds joined the Party – if they knew the right people. The Party was the fast track to a better life.

Although the CPC ranks are still growing, joining today offers fewer immediate benefits, and people's loyalty is to their families and their country before the Party. Even government itself is less about ideology and more about removing obstacles to rapid development.

Since different police officers and judges will state different regulations in their dealings with people, the first step for the Beijing authorities has been to attempt to create a uniform set of laws that everyone can recognise. China's reputation for corruption and producing counterfeit goods makes doing international business hard, so the authorities are now ordering more high profile arrests of corrupt officials. Civil rights are also improving; there are more discrimination and personal injury lawsuits passing the through the courts, and more patent lawyers protecting intellectual property.

Lei Feng

Before Deng Xiaoping's reforms, a good grasp of party ideology was important for personal advancement. The folk hero Lei Feng was a brave, self-sacrificing peasant held up as an example; today students still 'learn from Lei Feng'. 'Capitalist' business leaders were allowed to join the CPC only in 2002. Today, individual Beijingers control their own personal and professional lives, and even government officials can be non-Party members. Children still join the Young Pioneers and the Youth League, and do volunteer work on 5 March, Lei Feng Day, but these organisations are not as important as they used to be.

▼ The badge of the Mao Youth League is one use of symbolism in China's giant communist party propaganda, though today the CPC is less influential in everyday lives.

▲ Gateway leading to the offices of the Mayor of Beijing. Like much of government in China, the political offices of Beijing are shrouded in secrecy and security is always high.

Citizenship

Beijing's Mayor and nine Vice Mayors are elected in five-year terms. In addition Beijing has 4,403 deputies, also elected in five-year terms by the city's 2,336 electoral wards. But 'elections' can be misleading. Few non-party candidates are allowed to run for even lower office – many who try are hindered by unhelpful bureaucrats and mountains of red tape. Beijing has an official 95 per cent voter turnout rate but in fact no one actually seems to vote. There is little to choose between candidates that stand for election. However Beijing, and the rest of China, is experimenting with democracy. Residents' Committees (RCs) used to serve the residents of small areas, but were viewed by most people with suspicion as 'thought police'. Today, however, with more unemployment and fewer state services, people are looking for help. RCs are expanding their territories, from hundreds to thousands of households – and as more homes are threatened with destruction, more locals are using RCs to demand their rights as citizens.

◄ A community leader, signified by the red arm band, liaises between the local government and the community for which she is responsible.

Volunteerism

Volunteer work is new to China. Taking care of families was difficult enough, so helping strangers was never a priority. But families can only do so much, and nowadays, the State does less than ever. Wang Xingjuan started one of China's first Non-Governmental Organisations (NGOs), located in Beijing – the Maple Women's Counselling Centre. The centre helps victims of domestic violence, and runs a suicide hotline – a particularly high risk for Chinese women. Other volunteer-based organisations include Friends of Nature and Global Village Beijing, both based in Beijing, which work to raise awareness of the city's severe environmental problems (see p. 50). Groups such as Hua Dan, a theatre group that helps immigrant workers improve their self-esteem, and Magic Hospital, who provide free entertainment in Beijing's Children Hospital, have started to show Beijingers how volunteer work can benefit their communities, without the involvement of the city or national authorities.

▼ A passer-by reads a board appealing for blood donors. Volunteering is a relatively new concept in China.

National government

Tiananmen Square is home to China's most important buildings; The Forbidden City, Mao Zedong's Mausoleum, and the Great Hall of the People, the seat of the national legislature. Little information is available on what happens happens inside the Great Hall, but it is here that the laws of the nation are made. Officially, the Communist Party of China (CPC) and the government are two separate entities; but in practice there is little meaningful difference. Some national leaders have had different titles – Party Chairman, General Secretary, or President. For some time Deng Xiaoping's only title, despite being the unquestioned leader of China, was Honorary Chairman of the Chinese Contract Bridge Association! Currently, the leadership is divided under three titles: General Secretary of the Party, President of China, and Chairman of the Central Military Commission – and one leader does not necessarily hold all offices. Despite the mystery, however, Beijing citizens love to talk politics.

▼ The Great Hall of the People is the seat of the Chinese government.

Transport in Beijing

While Beijing is well-linked to large national and international cities, local transport services within the city are struggling to keep pace with the city's rapid development, creating a host of new problems. Many residents have turned to the car as an alternative to public transport, or the traditional bicycle, creating huge congestion and pollution problems.

▲ Passengers disembark from a regional airline. Internal air travel is growing rapidly in China and Beijing is a key hub in this network.

National links

An inland city, Beijing has no port but shares port services with the neighbouring city of Tianjin, another municipality, about 137 km to the east. The port handles 68 million tonnes of goods annually. Beijing is the centre of the national railway network, which is continuing to expand. On 1 July 2006, a luxury train route from Beijing to Tibet opened, and authorities are planning

▼ New trains are part of a massive investment in local and national rail services for Beijing and beyond.

a high-speed train to Shanghai. The city's new airport, due for completion by 2008, is said to be the world's largest. Beijing plans to open a second airport in 2010, this time in the underdeveloped southern area of the city.

Traffic

Car and traffic congestion has become an enormous problem in Beijing in a very short space of time. Beijing issues 2,000 new number plates daily – as many as Shanghai issues in a month. The two million cars on Beijing's roads in 2006 were seven years ahead of projections; current projections predict 3.5 million for 2008. Economically this is a good thing – for every one car sold, two jobs are created, but as car use increases ten per cent annually, road capacity only increases by two per cent. Today, just less than 30 per cent of Beijingers use the subway, which, with only three lines, does not have nearly enough capacity. Most major cities with subways share problems of capacity shortage and that is one reason that private vehicle use is increasing in cities like Beijing. Eight planned additional lines should ease the burden on the existing network and take some traffic off the roads as the drivers return to public transport. The government is also increasing urban and suburban railway transport capacity, and building more highways and parallel roads. Officials are also discussing a possible congestion tax, and a higher parking fee, up from the current US$0.12 per hour.

▶ Road traffic is becoming a major problem in Beijing, especially during rush hour when even major new roads with multiple lanes can grind to a halt.

CASE STUDY

Kong Fangchang, taxi driver

Kong Fangchang found taxi driving a welcome change from the monotony of a government electrician's job, but after 12 years, things are different, as traffic levels have risen enormously. "It's rush hour all day long," says Fangchang. Petrol prices have almost doubled, and the fleet of new taxis that the authorities say the drivers must use cost more to repair.

Another problem is the explosion of *hei che*, or illegal unlicensed taxis. Once a feature of only the remotest suburbs, these taxis have come into central areas. "Illegal taxis can wait in the areas taxis aren't allowed," says Fangchang, "and the police don't notice them. There's

only so much business out there, and they are getting a big piece of the pie." The rise in the number of illegal taxis and private cars also mean fewer people hailing taxis from the side of the road. As a consequence Fangchang's monthly income of US$248 keeps shrinking.

▲ Bicycles remain a popular mode of travel here during the morning rush hour, but the car is being given priority in many parts of the city as it is considered more 'modern'.

Car alternatives

Despite manufacturing more and more cars, China remains the world leader in bicycle production, making over 60 million annually. For most of the twentieth century Beijing was a city of bicycles, with millions of people using this healthy and environmentally safe form of transport. A popular innovation is the electric bicycle, which became illegal (but is still used) in January 2006. Beijing's government claimed the electric bicycles were unsafe, but critics say that officials feel that cars will better boost Beijing's 'developed city' image.

Informal transport alternatives

Beijing's informal transport economy is based on illegal taxis and motorcycles waiting for custom outside subway stations and in outlying neighbourhoods. More common are the *san lun che* (three-wheeled vehicles) for transporting either goods or people. These can be pedicabs, pulled by bicycles or mopeds, or open carts attached to 'tricycles'. Mule-drawn carts can be used to haul bricks at construction sites, or fruit around neighbourhoods.

▼ *San lun che* wait to carry rush hour commuters home from Shangdi urban railway station.

The bicycle culture

Bicycle safety equipment, while readily available, is rarely used, despite the heavy car traffic on the roads. Whole families can be seen weaving through traffic perched on a single bicycle with no light, one reflector, and a tiny bell. Cyclists seem more worried about weather than traffic, frequently wearing special gear to block sandstorms or sunlight. Good locks are important, however, as bicycle theft is common. Some riders pay 'bike watchers' outside shops to stand guard while they are inside, or buy very cheap bicycles that can be easily replaced. A popular bicycle is the steel *Fei Ge* (Flying Pigeon). Status symbols when they first appeared in the 1960s, they are still used today, but more modern racing and mountain bikes are used by wealthier Chinese.

▲ A bicycle watcher at a parking area for bikes outside a subway station.

CASE STUDY

Beijing for Bikes (B4B)

Many Chinese think that a first class city means cars, and bicycles make the city look poor. At the same time they will complain about pollution and traffic. Friends of Nature's Beijing for Bikes (B4B) initiative is trying to promote cycling as a healthy, sustainable transportation option, not an economic necessity. "Over half our pollution comes from our two million cars," says Hu Huizhe, director of B4B.

Beijing has wide, flat streets that form a city grid, and have bicycle lanes separated by a tree barrier – the perfect infrastructure for a cycling city. But as roads are widened to allow more car traffic, bicycle lanes get removed. Hu Huizhe organises bicycle publicity and awareness events, and campaigns for car-free zones in Beijing. "By 2008, traffic will be a big problem," Huizhe says, "and if we want to welcome guests from all over the world (for the Olympic Games), we have to make space for them."

Culture, leisure and tourism

Beijing is China's tourist capital. As the seat of power, the city has great appeal for many Chinese. For foreigners, Beijing combines a modern, diverse, international city with most of China's greatest cultural treasures.

The heart of the city

Tiananmen (Gate of Heavenly Peace) has been the spiritual centre of Beijing, and all China, since 1417, but it was Mao who built the world's largest public square, measuring 50 hectares, the size of 82 football pitches. Beijingers cong gate there to picnic and fly kites, even in winter, and foreigners visit because of its history. To the north of the square is the Forbidden City. Built in 1406, these 800 buildings with 9,000 rooms cover 720,000 sq m, and are nine times bigger than London's Millennium Dome. Other popular places include the architecturally stunning Temple of Heaven, completed in 1420, which was a place where the emperor prayed for good harvests, and the Summer Palace to the northwest of the city, which rings an enormous lake where boating trips are popular in the summer.

▼ The Imperial Vault of Heaven (*Huang Qiong Yu*) part of Tiantan Gongyuan, or the Temple of Heaven complex.

Other attractions

Just to the north of Beijing is the famous Great Wall (see p. 8). Construction and repair have been piecemeal over about 2000 years, but it was during the Ming Dynasty (1368-1644) where most of the sections were joined, and it assumed the form we know today. Built with brick, egg yolk and rice paste as a way to keep northern invaders out, it proved ineffective as protection, and isolated China from the world, which hindered its development. Today the parts of the Wall easily accessed from Beijing are a huge tourist draw, but visitors can also see the 'Wild Wall' in Beijing's suburbs. This is the unpaved Great Wall, with crumbling brick surrounded by silent forests. In summer, foreigners camp (illegally) in the guard towers, paying local villagers to deliver firewood and beer.

Many visitors to Beijing go to some of the local markets. Panjiaoyuan is 3,000 stalls of (mostly fake) antiques, while the Ya Show and Xiu Shui markets have rows of cheap clothing, jewellery and souvenirs.

Beijing has many popular shows, such as Chinese Acrobats, Kung Fu, or Peking Opera (*Jingju*), a 200-year old art form where storytelling combines speaking, singing, martial arts and elaborate makeup. More modern entertainment is also widely available, with bands and DJs to be seen in clubs and at music festivals. There is also a Beijing punk movement, and the contemporary art scene (see p. 35) is becoming more popular every passing year.

▲ A trader reaches for a porcelain vase to show a customer at the 'antique market' at Panjiaoyuan, east of the second ring road.

▶ Keen followers of the Beijing punk movement.

Sports and leisure

For a city with such stifling air pollution and notoriously bad weather, Beijing has a great deal of outdoor activity. The Chinese believe in taking physical exercise to maintain balance (known as *yin* and *yang*). Beijing families go hiking in the mountains, and boating or swimming illegally in city lakes. Many residential areas have playgrounds in public places. Basketball is very popular – most Chinese boys believe playing basketball will make them taller. Running is rare, but badminton and skipping rope are very popular.

Other less strenuous activities include playing Chinese chess on street corners, and *wei qi* (the game known as *go* in Japan) in teahouses. Some people do *tai chi* or traditional fan dances in the parks.

Beijing's growing middle class is interested less in *tai chi*, and more in golf, scuba diving, and flying lessons. At a nearby reservoir, city-dwellers do weekend paragliding off surrounding hills, while not far away, shepherds look after their flocks. Wealthier and younger Chinese are more

▲ Kite flying is a popular activity. On the bridge that spans Kunming Lake at the Summer Palace, a kite flyer launches his butterfly kites into the blue sky.

conscious of their physical appearance than their health, and may exercise to maintain their weight, not 'balance'.

▼ Fan dancers in Ri Tan park.

Organised sports

Beijing's dense population and limited space means there are few community sport organisations. Coaches do recruit school children for teams; interested students attend training centres for swimming, gymnastics, table tennis or other sports. The best athletes may eventually join national or army teams, and for poorer children this may provide a route to a free education.

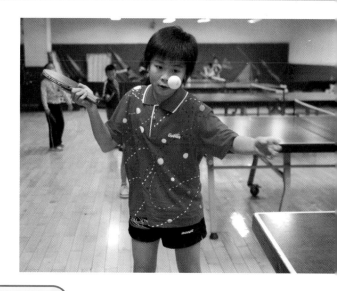

▶ Talent is often spotted early and the best athletes receive strong encouragement from the authorities.

CASE STUDY

Yang Hong Jin, Ambassador of Athletics

As Programme Director of the Beijing International Sports Centre, former weightlifter Yang Hong Jin organises sports exchanges between amateur Chinese and Western teams. Athletes get to enjoy sightseeing and friendly competition, and learn about cultural differences. "China and America have different training systems," Yang says. "In China, the children are selected at a very young age, and training is free. But then they get lazy. In America they have to pay for training," he continues, "so they want to do it."

Leisure sports have a very short history in China; even in the 1980s, training was for competition only. Yang feels that most Chinese exercise for health, rather than beauty, and, with the exception of the upper class, that attitude will stay. "But now I think people are experiencing the side effects of being rich, such as eating too much," he says, referring to Beijing's growing problem with obesity. But Yang feels it's all part of development. "Maybe some people have to die before other people realise there's a problem."

The business of tourism

China is now the world's third most popular tourist destination, and is expected to reach number one in 2020. But travellers still encounter a lot of *mafan* (trouble). Arranging tickets, hotels and reservations can be prohibitively difficult, and tourist scams are on the rise. Beijing has a love-hate relationship with tourism. The Chinese that work at tourist sites can seem pushy, aggressive and rude, but Westerners buying fruit from a local market or mule cart can be embarrassed at how little they pay.

▲ Rickshaw drivers wait for tourist trade in the *hutong* areas surrounding Houhai Lake. Tourism is providing many new employment opportunities.

Preserving the culture

The tourist industry supports some illicit activities, such as the illegal taxis and unlicensed tour guides found near palaces and temples, but there are positives, too. In 2000, the city government was planning to demolish most of the old city's *siheyuan/hutong* housing (see p.26). However, these areas were exactly what foreigners wanted to see. Areas that had been earmarked for destruction became tourist attractions, with *hutong* tours, restaurants, hotels, and coffee shops with wireless Internet. The emphasis on tourism gave *siheyuan* owners a new source of income. However some Beijingers feel that turning a *siheyuan* into a coffee shop with wireless Internet access isn't preserving Chinese culture. Opinions differ as to which is better, preserving traditional housing to appeal to Western tourists, or tearing it down altogether and building high-rises to house Beijing's expanding population. Tourism is saving the buildings, but no one knows if it's really saving the culture.

▼ Visitors to the Forbidden City are dressed in traditional court costume to have their photograph taken.

Shi TaoTao and tea culture

Like many middle class Chinese, Shi TaoTao was a reluctant accountancy student, as accountancy has long been considered a fast track to a good job. She took up film editing for fun, and became a documentary filmmaker for China Education Television (CETV). "All my interviews were in tea houses," she explains. "I like the tea culture, but not the teahouses. I knew my teahouse would be better." Bored with television, Taotao studied tea culture and rented a space across from the Confucian Temple on Beijing's oldest street. "I wanted to create a centre for Chinese culture." Her tea ceremony uses the same movements as everyone else's, but

she incorporates Tang Dynasty poetry and Confucian sayings – in Chinese, English and Japanese. Her teahouse plays traditional Chinese music, not Western muzak on Chinese instruments. In the afternoons it's filled with Western temple visitors; in the evenings, it's host to Chinese artists, actors, poets, Confucian scholars, and Buddhist monks. "Tea culture is over 5,000 years old," she says. "If you study tea history, you know Chinese history."

◀ An employee prepares tea samples for customers to taste at a shop in 'Tea Street', an area in Beijing dedicated to the retail and wholesale of teas from all over China.

The Beijing environment

Beijing suffers from both natural and manmade environmental problems. Its arid climate makes it vulnerable to sandstorms and perpetual water shortage, while its rapid development creates pollution, and strains what few resources it has. Fortunately, experts are starting to take action – and because of the 2008 Olympics the Beijing government is listening.

Sandstorms

Wars, land misuse, over-population and rapid urbanisation have all caused the haphazard clearing of trees in the area around Beijing, leading to desertification and soil erosion, which costs China US$6.5-9.1 billion every year in lost agricultural revenue. Sand dunes 70 km to the north are slowly drifting south towards the city, and serious storms have blown sand from north China to Korea, Japan, and even as far as California.

In response to the problem, farming has been regulated, and the government has reforested 44,560 hectares of land in northern China. The 66,700 hectares of trees planted between Beijing and the neighbouring city of Tianjin should absorb 15,000,000 tonnes of sand annually.

Pollution

A bigger problem than sand and dust storms is the production of the pollutants sulphur dioxide and nitrous oxide, from factories, coal stoves, and cars. Major industrial pollution is decreasing but car emissions are getting worse, due both to increased private car ownership and to rising global oil prices – China now buys cheaper and more polluting 'sour oil' with a higher level of sulphur.

Local experts insist the city's air is better, and skies are bluer – a 32.5 per cent decrease in pollutants in 2004 from 1998, but, by the middle of the day, a dirty dishwater-coloured haze obscures the view of buildings and the mountains. Beijing now has the reputation of being one of the most polluted cities in the world.

▲ Street sweepers struggle to keep pace with the amount of dust in the Beijing environment generated by sand storms and the present construction boom.

▲ Smoggy morning traffic on Beijing's busy second ring road.

Wang Xiamen and green rooftops

As an aeronautical engineer, then a philosophy professor, Wang Xiamen never felt that he achieved anything. Now, as Secretary-General of China Environment Protection Foundation (CEPF), he is landscaping Beijing's roofs. "Roof gardens absorb dust particles, purify the air, protect roofs, conserve energy, and improve drainage," he explains. Plants absorb glare and city noise, and serve as natural insulation – saving cities tens of millions in energy costs. Roof gardens also combat the "urban heat island" effect. "Large scale landscaping can lower city temperatures by five degrees in the summer," says Wang. And at US$18.50 per sq m, it's cheaper than relocating factories.

Green rooftop projects also provide neighbourhoods with much needed business, employment and volunteer opportunities – and Wang feels he's finally making a contribution. "When I retired, I thought staying home would make me crazy," he said. Now 65, he visits worksites and climbs buildings. "I'm doing a good thing, and I'm making a little money," he says. "I'm happy."

▲ Wang Xiamen standing in a completed garden on top of a government building created by the China Environmental Protection Foundation's Green Rooftop Landscape Project.

The climate

Beijing has hot summers and very cold, dry winters. The average temperature in January is -5°C, but they have been recorded as low as -23°C. The highest recorded summer temperature is 43°C, and coupled with high humidity and poor air quality, such conditions can make life in the city very uncomfortable.

▶ Average temperatures and rainfall for Beijing.

Rainfall (mm)

Temperature

Dry Beijing

In 1949 the Miyun reservoir was built to supply enough drinking water to the cities of Beijing and Tianjin and also Hebei province. The Miyun, and also the Guanting, reservoirs could provide 3 billion cubic metres of water – and an additional 15 reservoirs constructed in the following years should have ensured that no one went thirsty.

▶ The Yongding River dried up when a reservoir was built nearby and redirected the water. Beijing has relied on redirecting water to meet its needs, but the long term environmental effects could be disastrous.

No more water

Today, most of those reservoirs are polluted or have dried up. Miyun and Guanting together yield only 500 million cubic metres. Water use has increased dramatically in Beijing with domestic use alone almost doubling from 65 litres per person per day in 1988, to over 120 litres by 2001. This forces Beijing to divert water from the arid Hebei and Shanxi provinces – which have none to spare. Industry continues to use groundwater, which causes subsidence as the ground dries out, damaging city buildings, and experts think many water tables will be drained down to bedrock by 2016.

Beijing's population has grown by 11 million since 1949. Continued development of the city means both further construction and an increase in heavy industry, both of which consume and pollute water. As the incomes of the people of Beijing have risen, so has their demand for water. Furthermore, leaky transport pipes waste over 20 per cent of all transferred water.

◀ Pressure on water supplies means that extravagant uses such as washing cars could soon become more costly as prices go up.

The solution

Beijing is now imposing fines on polluters, distributing free taps that reduce water use, recycling more water, and discussing raising water prices to discourage overuse. A massive North-South Transfer Project will bring water from the water-rich Hubei province 1000 km to the south to the parched northeast. In spite of its cost (US$58 billion) and the relocation of 400,000 people along its route, experts see this as the only viable long term solution. The project will see three major canals, each over 1,300 km long, linking the major rivers of China with the dry lands of the north. The main central canal should be providing water to Beijing after 2010, but the whole project is not due for completion until the middle of the century, by which time the canals should supply the

▲ The building of new canals similar to this one on the outskirts of Beijing will help to alleviate the city's water shortages.

north of China with 44.8 billion cubic metres of water a year.

Not all action to ensure water supplies needs to be on a giant scale. Local citizenship action can also help. In 2001 a soy sauce factory was polluting the historically important Houhai Lake. A group of 23 residents took pictures, interviewed locals, confronted factory management and began a letter-writing campaign to local government, which eventually relocated the polluting factory. Remarkably, these concerned citizens were 11 years old.

CASE STUDY

World Wildlife Foundation's Education Initiative for Water

World Wildlife Foundation's (WWF) Education Initiative for Water (EIW) is the future of environmental education and the brainchild of Zhang Yi, WWF's Education Programme Officer. But water is just the beginning. "It's about introducing a new way of teaching and learning," she says. "The teachers use the water and community as a context for teaching. Traditionally in China, teachers talk and students listen. We're trying to teach another way."

Nature-loving Zhang Yi received a Master of Science degree in Environmental and Developmental Education before coming to WWF. "For the past eight years I've been trying to promote education for sustainable development, and put it in the schools," she says. EIW has been a success

with students, parents, and especially teachers. "They love being on an equal level with students," says Zhang. "There's a lot they can explore together." But even more important is citizen development. "We're teaching people how to take action to improve the environment."

Wastewater and recycling

Until the North-South Transfer Project is fully completed (see p. 53), Beijing, which runs out of useable water every ten months, will need to continue to divert water from neighbouring provinces. In an attempt to slow the rate of this water diversion, several different steps are being taken. Polluted lakes, rivers and reservoirs are being cleaned. The recycling of wastewater is also starting. Beijing could extract between 69 and 147 million tonnes from rainfall, and 645 million tonnes from recycled wastewater each year.

Wastewater treatment

The Jingcheng Recycled Water Company produces 495,000 cubic metres of water daily, but wastewater treatment plants use three to four tonnes of raw water to create one tonne of purified water. Having inefficient wastewater treatment plants means large amounts of wastewater is discharged without being treated, polluting rivers and groundwater. Beijing's water usage is only ten per cent recycled water, compared with 50 per cent in developed countries. Untreated wastewater pollutes soil and groundwater; repairing the damage costs twenty times more than preventing the problem.

But wastewater technology is a rapidly growing field, attracting a wide range of both experts and investment. Beijing is constructing new plants, improving existing technology, and fixing leaky pipelines. By 2008, China's capital will be treating 90 per cent of its urban sewage, and using 50 per cent recycled water.

▼ A couple sorts through waste and separates it into different materials for transport to a recycling centre, where they will sell it for reuse.

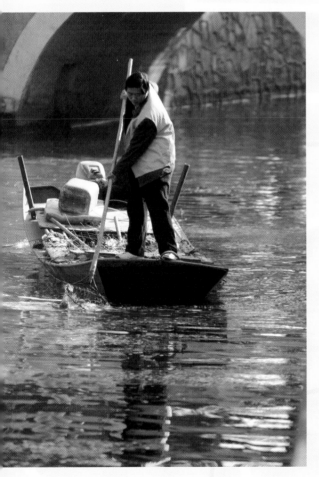

▲ A cleaner skims Houhai Lake for surface pollution as part of a clean-up of the city's waste. Water quality has been declining as the city has grown.

Household waste

The 15 million people in Beijing create mountains of household waste – 1.1 million tonnes annually in the central urban areas alone. Besides taking up space, untreated trash in landfills causes serious soil and groundwater pollution. Recycling programmes today consists largely of elderly people sifting through garbage cans, or migrant workers circling neighbourhoods, calling for refuse. But Beijing has begun waste-sorting programmes and is building 1,800 recycling stations, planning for a 30 per cent recycle rate by 2008.

▶ A recycling station where waste is separated into its various materials for reprocessing and sale.

CASE STUDY

Dr Zhang Huichun, wastewater treatment

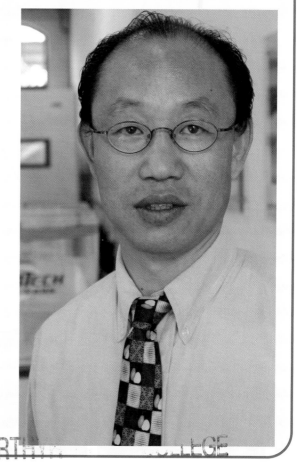

"If you want a sustainable economy, you can't pollute the environment," says Dr Zhang Huichun, owner of Greentech Engineering. Zhang, who has degrees in Hydrogeology, Hydraulics and Environmental Studies, uses biomass to treat wastewater and destroy pollutants.

"You grow a special kind of bacteria, depending on the type of waste," says Zhang. "The bacteria eats the pollutants and eventually sinks to the bottom." Treated water is drained off the surface; the remaining bacteria, or sludge, is dried, compressed into cakes, and sold as fertilizer, fuel or even building materials. Technology is racing ahead, one reason the environmental field is known as a 'morning business' in China, and holds special appeal for Zhang. "Business is challenging," he says. "But to be involved with something growing so fast, and that's also good for the environment, that's ideal. After all," he continues, "If you have a lot of money, but no drinking water, your standard of living will suffer."

The Beijing of tomorrow

For the Chinese government, Beijing, as China's international showcase, must be seen to be prosperous, open, and developed. As China's seat of national power, it should remain stable, controlled, and above all, Chinese. Blending these elements is difficult enough, but add in a large and dense population, haphazard development, very bad pollution and a shortage of natural resources, and Beijing's future might look bleak. Much like the Chinese Yin and Yang idea of balance, Beijing must balance its many opposing forces to prosper in a globalised world.

2008 Olympics

The Chinese are proud of their long, glorious history, and ashamed of their current underdeveloped status. Rapid economic growth is not enough; the country needs to prove that it is a global player, worthy of the world's respect. That opportunity is coming, with the 2008 Olympics.

Beijing's desire to show it's 'as good as the West' caused development to go into overdrive. But by-products such as pollution and water shortages could mean future economic hardship, and as more national resources are diverted to Beijing, more unemployed workers will follow. Forced relocation and a skyrocketing cost of living means that many Beijingers are pushed to society's outer edges, even as the economy continues to grow.

Sustainable development

Beijing's current pattern of consumption is not sustainable. The city can't build roads fast enough to add 2,000 new cars a week. Beijing can't keep taking water from local agricultural areas to supply a city that allows health spas and golf courses unlimited water supplies. In an important and significant change the Beijing

▼ The countdown to the Beijing Olympics of 2008 has proven a major stimulus to a wide range of developments in the city.

▲ A mother and daughter walk across Tiananmen Square on 5 November 2005, the smoggiest day ever recorded in Beijing at the time. Such days are a clear warning that Beijing cannot continue to develop unchecked.

authorities are listening to their people – holding public hearings and consulting with experts, engaging in free debate and experimentation, and supporting grassroots environmental movements. Beijing's desire for international credibility has caused some decisions to be taken without proper consideration, but has also led to closer observation of Western problems – and their solutions.

Beijing megalopolis

Some of Beijing's short-term goals include increasing both the private and service sector's percentage of the city's GDP, as well as doubling the actual number, and increasing people's disposable income. Long-term plans are more ambitious, however. One of Tiananmen Square's most popular attractions is the giant Olympic clock, counting down to 2008. But some look to the Beijing Megalopolis of 2020, the future home to 18 million people. The plan is to transform today's satellite towns into 11 urbanised cities, with universities, high quality hospitals, theatres and sports stadiums, as well as hi-tech industries and factories, and rail lines for those who still need to commute. The key is to keep all areas diverse, with people of different jobs and incomes living together, so one area isn't vacated even as another prospers. The Megalopolis won't change the face of central Beijing, but it will ease the burden on resources and ensure further sustainable development for the city, in the twenty-first century and beyond.

▲ Huairou, an hour-and-a-half drive northeast of Beijing city centre is one of the new satellite areas that form Beijing's vision of the future.

Glossary

Autonomous Regions In China, these are similar to provinces, but have a higher concentration of minority peoples.

Chinese New Year This is China's most important holiday. Because travel is so expensive, this is often the only time families can get together.

Communist A person, party or government that follows the political theory which advocates a society where all property is shared, and people work and are paid according to their ability and need.

Confucian Relating to the Chinese philosopher Confucius (551-479 BC), who had a strong influence on Asian culture.

Desertification When previously fertile land becomes desert because of drought, deforestation or poor farming methods.

Intellectual property A work or invention that is the result of creativity, such as a design or manuscript, which may be protected by patent or copyright law.

Land Redistribution Programme During the Cultural Revolution, Mao tried to create a more equal society. Anyone with a large home was forced to share with two or three other families.

Mainlanders Chinese who live on Mainland China, not Hong Kong, Macau or Taiwan.

Nitrous Oxide One of the many gasses found in automotive exhaust.

Non-Governmental Organisation (NGO) An organisation not belonging to, affiliated with, or receiving money from any government.

Reparations Making amends for a wrong one has done by payment or other means, usually done by the losing side of a war.

Research and Development (R & D) In industry, work directed towards the innovation, introduction and improvement of products and processes.

Satellite cities A smaller city closely connected to a larger, neighbouring city, designed to encourage people to move out of the city centre, and ease congestion.

Special Economic Zone A region whose economic laws are different than the country's economic laws (usually tax breaks for foreign investment).

Sulphur dioxide Another pollutant found in car exhaust.

Tai Chi Chinese system of slow meditative physical exercise designed for relaxation, achieving balance and health.

Tea Ceremony Called cha dao in Chinese, this refers to the traditional movements, sayings and culture associated with drinking certain types of tea.

Warlords Usually a regional military commander with his own army and individual autonomy.

World Trade Organisation (WTO) An international body founded in 1995 to promote international development and economic development by reducing tariffs and other restrictions.

Yin and Yang The traditional Chinese black and white circle symbol, which represents balance.

Further information

Websites

www.lonelyplanet.com
Good for travel and cultural information.

www.en.beijing2008.com
The official Beijing Olympic website.

www.thebeijingguide.com
This site offers panoramic shots of Beijing sights.

www.ebeijing.gov.cn/default.htm
The official Beijing city website.

Books

Insight Guide: China Scott Rutherford, Langenscheldt Publishers, Ninth Edition, 2002.

Lonely Planet Beijing Damian Harper, Lonely Planet Publications, Sixth Edition, 2005.

Rough Guide to Beijing Simon Lewis, Rough Guides Publications, Second Edition, 2004.

Culture Shock! China: A Guide to Customs and Etiquette Kevin Sinclair and Iris Wong Po-Yee, Graphic Arts Centre Publishing Company, Expanded edition, 2002.

The Chinese Have a Word for it: The Complete Guide to Chinese Thought and Culture Boyd Lafayette De Mente, McGraw Hill, 2000.

Things Chinese Du Feibao and Du Bai, China Travel and Tourism Press, 2002.

Old Beijing: People, Houses and Lifestyles Xu Chengbei, Foreign Language Press 2001.

Old Beijing: In the Shadow of the Imperial Throne Xu Chengbei, Foreign Language Press, 2001.

A Treasury of China's Wisdom: A Story Book for Everyone Chinghua Tang Foreign Language Press, 1996

Red China Blues: My Long March from Mao to Now Jan Wong, Anchor, 1997

Wild Swans: Three Daughters of China by Jung Chang, Touchstone, reprinted 2003.

Index